SPLIT

By Marcus Brotherton
MULTNOMAH PUBLISHERS® *SISTERS, OREGON*

FLIPSWITCH WARNING

FS This book may contain thought-provoking content you probably didn't hear in Sunday school. It should be discussed and debated with family and friends. This book does not contain the answers to all your questions, but helps you ask the right questions. Some biblical material may be inappropriate and shocking for people who want to be comfortable.

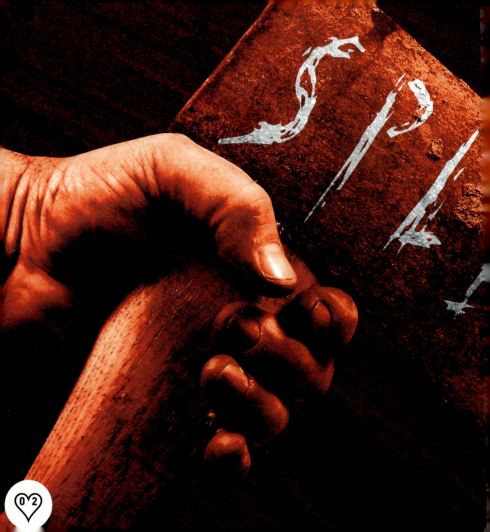

Downward

with incredible speed
rushes a heavy
iron axe
toward the
top of my head
so close now I feel it
splitting me jagged and scarring
like green firewood **WHACK**

http://www.splitblog.com/savannahkid46/a

Name: Savannah   Savannahkid46

Interests: bright colors, ring fingers, good music, sunny days, horror movies, and milkshakes (mmm...milkshakes)

Expertise: being pretty average at alotta things, mostly :)

My thoughts for today: April 5

Last night my parents told me they were splitting up. They haven't been seperated or anything. It came as a complete shock. They went out to dinner and when they came home they told me they're through. They said their marriage takes too much work. I sat for a long time in the kitchen just looking at them then I cried. I had a million questions. Did I have anything to do with this? what happens next? Then I cried some more. They said they both lead individual lives and putting them together takes to much work. They both think a marriage counselor isn't worth it. So this is it. I feel so low right now.

> "All I can do is watch them fall apart
> While they say there's no other way.
> There's got to be a better choice
> When this one causes so much pain."
> "Split" by Miserable Now

SPLIT!

*This moment,
life has just changed.*

*Somebody you love tells you
they're getting divorced.*

*You always remember...this moment.
It doesn't matter if they've been divorced
for two days or ten years.*

*In this moment, life has changed.
Their life and your life.
Forever.*

FOREVER.

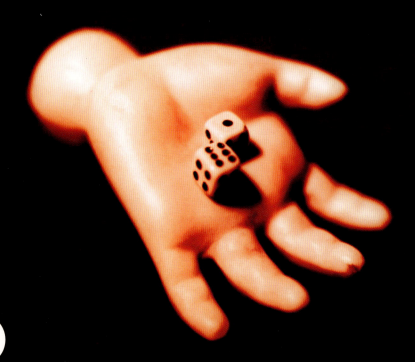

─ Quint Tairenteenodale Productions Presents ─

SPLITTIN' EVERYTHING
THE GAME SHOW NOBODY WANTS TO WIN

WELCOME, KIDS OF **DIVORCED PARENTS**, to "SPLITTIN' EVERYTHING! The Game Show Nobody Wants to Win." I'm your host, Quint Tairenteenodale. Because you're here today, it means your parents have just split up, and guess what—you've already won this crazy game!

Announcer **JOHNNY FILBERT**, tell them about their prizes, which are as exciting as my ever-immovable hairpiece…

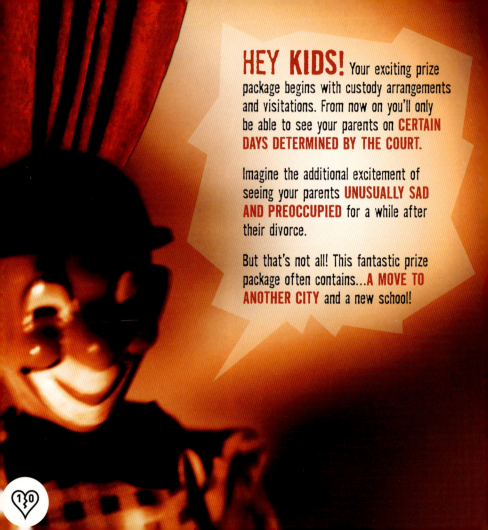

Imagine the fun of being challenged with concentrating in this new environment—**YOUR GRADES MAY EVEN TAKE A NEVER-BEFORE-SEEN DIP** for a while.

But don't worry, your parent's new emotions will mirror your roller-coaster grades as they experience the wild and crazy world of dating again. That's right, imagine **THE JOY OF MEETING YOUR PARENTS' NEW SIGNIFICANT OTHERS.** (Their dates will be refreshingly simple, as all family finances will be strained.)

And did we mention family holidays? Christmas? Birthdays? **NEVER THE SAME AGAIN!**

That's it—that's what you've won! Enjoy your prize package on **"SPLITTIN' EVERYTHING!** The Game Show Nobody Wants to Win."

http://www.splitblog.com/savannahkid46/a

Name: Savannah   Savannahkid46

Friends: MeSoCrunchy, Moffat, Danni Dynomite, Careoooke101, Clintman, AlannaSHAMA, Angel, Ruby Tuesday, Mandi Apple, Davislovecuprocks, ClaraBoBearaXYZ

commentsfromfriends

Comments from friends: April 3

My parents divorced three years ago. Everybody hears a lot of the same stuff when their parents split up. "We still love you." "Things just didn't work out." "We drifted apart." "We just don't love each other anymore." What you're going through is right on track. Sorry you've got to go through that junk. Okay, true 'dat. Double tru!

—MeSoCrunchy

I remember when my parents divorced, it was like the whole world went crazy for me. Mostly I remember how in the dark I felt. I was 13, old enough to know a lot of things, but I had no clue what went on between my parents. They were different people in front of me than they were behind closed doors, so I never knew stuff. I would get little snippets of information here and there, but never anything concrete. Just mysterious.

—Moffat

i totally blamed myself when they separated. in my eyes, the only connection between my parents was me—so the divorce must have had something to do with me. but it doesn't. it doesn't. it doesn't. it doesn't.

—Danni Dynomite

MIDWAY CAFÉ

Movie Proposal no. 416: A film by Earl Danglemeyer Jr.

Plot Summary: A coming-of-age high school angst film where a bunch of kids sit around in an all-night diner and talk about life...

Idea in a nutshell: Sort of like *Party of Five* meets *The OC* meets *Sixteen Candles* meets *Dawson's Creek* meets *Rebel Without a Cause* meets *Beverly Hills, 90210* meets *The Partridge Family* meets *Doogie Howser, MD*. (You know, something really original.)

Scene 14: at The Diner, 1 a.m.
[group is sitting at booth waiting for food to come]

NESSA: What did you order, Iago, a double burger and fries again?

IAGO: Nah, I'm running track this spring. I had to sell my saxophone to pay for my track shoes, though. Mom took off to Vegas and left us. My stupid alcoholic dad wouldn't spring for the bucks. I'm actually relieved my parents got divorced. There's just less tension in the house now. Can you imagine that? Divorce always sucks, but not everybody is completely bummed that their parents got divorced. How crazy is that? I wonder if divorce is actually the best thing that ever happened in my crummy house.

MARLON: Hmmmph. Parents.

NESSA: (moves closer to Marlon) Parents? Does anybody actually have two parents anymore?

GEMMA: (head down, mumbling) Not me. There haven't been two cars in the garage at my house for a long time. Dad dumped Mom to be with his younger, better-looking secretary. It's so cliché. That's why I turned to punk music and black eyeliner. Because that's certainly not cliché. The truth is—when people get hurt, they often act out in ways that are deemed unacceptable to society. That's what I'm all about.

But I'm getting ahead of myself right now—you'll have to figure this out as we keep talking. I might even create a collage right here at The Diner—maybe a snow scene to illustrate my inner hurt where I shake down dandruff from my head.

DRAKE: (inches closer to Gemma) Would anybody like some Certs? I wish I only had two parents. I actually have six parents, I guess. My parents divorced when I was a baby, then both got remarried, then divorced again, then remarried. Every pairing had kids. So I have real siblings, half siblings, siblings that are related to some but not others. Trying to celebrate holidays together as a family is completely impossible. Me—I'm just going to avoid it all and never getting married. With all the divorce and remarriage I've experienced I'm convinced there's no way anybody can have a good marriage.

NESSA: Yeah, I sure hope you're wrong. [looks longingly at Marlon] The food is here. Let's eat. [voice becomes sexy] Hey Marlon...would you like to share some of my fries?

MARLON: (holds hands with Nessa under table)
Sure baby. We all just want to be loved. Isn't that what divorce is about in the first place? It's kind of mixed up, backwards. People want to be loved—and they're not getting that—so they bail to find love somewhere else.

and... —SCENE—

http://www.splitblog.com/savannahkid46/a

Name: Savannah Savannahkid46

Interests: bright colors, ring fingers, good music, sunny days, horror movies, and milkshakes (mmm...milkshakes)

Expertise: being pretty average at alotta things, mostly :)

Currently playing:

"Today Is Not Fit" by *Cowgill*

currentlyplaying/todayisnotfit/

My thoughts for today: April 5

My parents said I have to decide who I want to live with. I've got three days to make the decision. What do I do? Go with my mom or my dad. No matter who I choose one of them is going to be hurt for sure. maybe it sounds stupid, but I just want to be held like a small baby and wrapped up in a warm blanket…

To: Savannahkid46@jmail.com
From: Hemorix@jmail.com

Hey Savannah,

I read your blog, and, man, that's a tough one. I don't know what you should do. There is so much to sort through when your parents get divorced. In some ways, you've got it lucky. At least your parents made a clean break of it. I remember just before my parents got divorced when I was 12 I kept this sort of detached report in my diary about what I overheard at night in our house. It went something like this:

1:34 a.m. Gravel crunching in driveway. Front door opens? Hope it's Dad. Might be Brian, though, coming over to "comfort" Mom. Yeah right.

1:51 a.m. Whispers. Something gets bumped, dumb giggles down the hall. That would have to be Brian...

So maybe I knew too much? Who knows? My Mom and Dad actually came out and told me once that they didn't love each other anymore. I guess that's truth, but sometimes I wonder how much of the truth kids need to hear? All I know is that divorce is sad. It's sad for everybody. It's sad for your mom and dad. It's sad for their parents. It's sad for you and your sister. I don't think anyone plans for their marriage to end when they get married. That's what's so sad about divorce. People are sad because they've lost their love. In terms of who you should live with, I don't know. I'm really sorry. That's a tough one.

Love ya babe,
Hemorix

WHAT'S YOUR EXPERIENCE?

WHACK! If you're reading this, there's a good chance either your parents are divorced (or are thinking about getting a divorce), or else one of your good friends' parents is going through a divorce. ***WHACK!*** Probably there's a lot of uncertainty in your life right now. ***WHACK!*** You wonder what to say. ***WHACK!*** Maybe you (or your friend) are going back and forth between parents. ***WHACK!*** Maybe you're living with one of your parents and your parent's new partner. ***WHACK!*** Maybe you're dealing with new stepbrothers and stepsisters or new half-brothers or sisters. ***WHACK!***

When you're dealing with a SPLIT, it's common to feel a bunch of crazy, mixed up emotions. It's like the axe just keeps falling, again and again. And you feel...

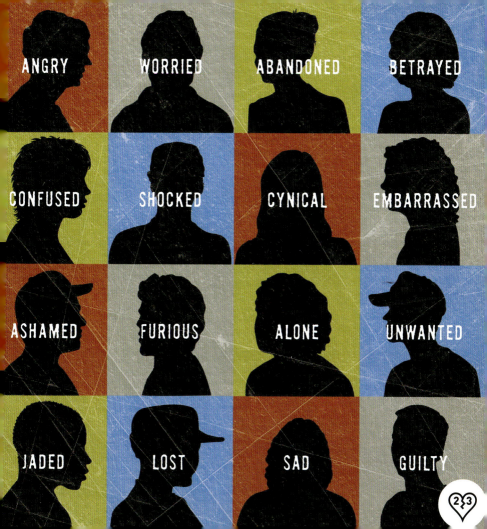

SO WHAT DO YOU DO? OR HOW COULD YOU HELP YOUR FRIEND THROUGH THIS? HOW DO YOU DEAL WITH THE PAIN OF A SPLIT?

The axe CRASHED
through me
STEEL
COLD FORCE
I am two pieces now
There has to be a way
to get through this
a way to
hold things
together

I just have to find it
But I dont know if I can...

FLIP HERE

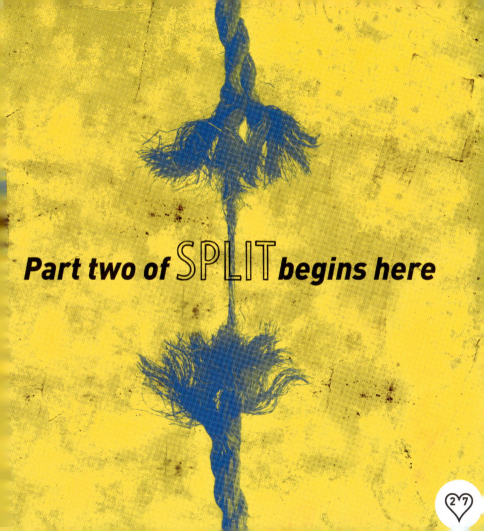

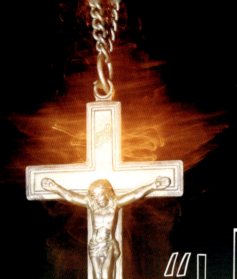

*Think divorce sucks?
God agrees with you...*

"I HATE DIVORCE,"

says the LORD God of Israel—Malachi 2:16

Right up front... it's important not to miss this:

When God says He hates divorce, He hates it because of what you're feeling right now.

He doesn't hate divorced people, or parents who are divorcing (and maybe behaving badly right now), or kids whose parents are divorced or divorcing (and perhaps also behaving badly right now).

Know this: When you experience a divorce in any way, God doesn't love you less or have any less than His best in mind for you.

God hates divorce, but never the people affected by a divorce.

So what do you do? Sometimes when you experience a SPLIT, it feels like you have sorrow in your heart every day. What do you do then?

The simple answer (but the really complex answer too) is that you *feel*. Sometimes we get the idea that Jesus didn't have any feelings. Or that He had only nice, holy feelings. On the contrary, Jesus experienced all feelings, and He invites us to come to Him with all of ours.

We don't have a priest who is out of touch with our reality. [Jesus has] been through weakness and testing, experienced it all—all but the sin.
Hebrews 4:15
(The Message)

Jesus was frustrated when family members didn't understand him. (John 2:3-4) Jesus was furious when his father's house was dishonored. (John 2:16) Jesus wept when he felt sorrow. (John 11:35)

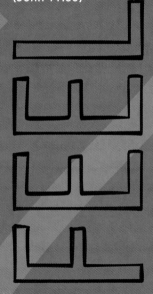

ONE COOL THING ABOUT JESUS IS THIS...

Jesus doesn't try to cheer you up when you feel like screaming. Jesus doesn't just sort of shrug things off or try to convince you that you're not raging inside. Jesus never just sort of grins at you and tells you to just "buck up." Jesus respects you enough to let you truly feel what you feel...

But what happens if you do try to stuff your feelings?

The hottest boy band around
(for the past week, anyway)

Dudley

←← PRESENTS →→

"never talk, think, trust"

a song about stuffing your true feelings (and what happens when you do)

Devon Dudley
age 14, Singer
Writing songs since age 14.
Likes long hair, video games, girls, and hairdryers.

Denver Dudley
age 10, Drummer
Likes long hair, video games, skateboarding, mouthing off, bubblegum, and hair gel.

Dylan Dudley
age 17, Bass player
Likes long hair, video games, girls, Ferraris, hair gel, hair dryers, shampoo, and barrettes.

Dooley Dudley
age 15, Guitar player
Likes long hair, video games, snowboarding, girls, and conditioner.

http://www.splitblog.com/savannahkid46/th

Name: Savannah Savannahkid46

Friends: MeSoCrunchy, Moffat, Danni Dynomite, Careoooke101, Clintman, AlannaSHAMA, Angel, Ruby Tuesday, Mandi Apple, Davislovecuprocks, ClaraBoBearaXYZ

 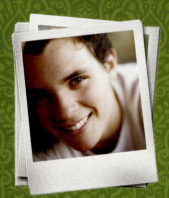 

oponder/april7blog/commentsfromfriends

Savannah's thoughts to ponder: April 7

There's another thing...what I don't get is this. Divorce is so unfair. unfair, unfair, unfair. I didn't ask for this. how come I'm forced to deal with my parents' mistakes?!

Comments from friends:

I'm really sorry about your folks' divorce. My parents divorced more than 10 years ago. Life is probably really painful for you right now. I know it was for me. As funny as it sounds, it's okay for life to not feel good. Actually, it shouldn't feel good right now. Just let yourself feel miserable for awhile. Knowing that it's okay to do that, helps.

—AlannaSHAMA

I remember the night when my parents said they were getting divorced, I just went into my parents' bedroom and I cried forever. I hadn't cried like that since I was a little kid.

—Clintman

When my dad left, it's like the whole house was empty. We turned the TV on a lot more, I think just because the house didn't seem as lonely. It was always on. But then I started turning it off. To me, it felt like we should feel empty. That's what was really happening.

—Davislovecuprocks

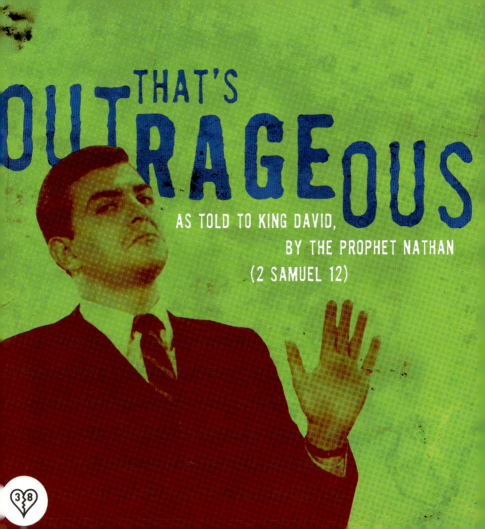

Once, there were two men, one rich and the other poor. The rich man had huge numbers of sheep and cattle. But the poor man had nothing but one little female lamb. He raised it, and it grew up with him and his children. The lamb shared his food, drank from his cup, and even slept in his arms. It was like a daughter to him.

Now, a traveler came to the rich man, but instead of taking one of his own sheep or cattle to prepare a meal for the traveler, the rich man stole the lamb that belonged to the poor man and....

UNFAIR

feels like something precious to you was stolen, killed, destroyed.

UNFAIR

feels like your life is bloody and battered, in a million pieces.

And it's easy to stay stuck in UNFAIR for a long, long time. (Hey, you have every right to.) But you'll just end up losing. Somewhere along the line—hopefully sooner rather than later—you've gotta deal with the UNFAIR.

UN FAIR

is you dealing with:

HURT SORROW CONFUSION SADNESS LOSS RAGE PAIN

Here's something you might not want to hear...

Lambs do get SPLATTERED

SORRY.

There's nothing razz-a-ma-tazz about that...
Nothing hopeful or helpful or happy...
Just that one stark, cold fact...

LIFE IS UNFAIR.

Joseph got thrown in prison when he didn't do anything wrong. (Genesis 39)
Stephen had rocks heaved at him when he didn't do anything wrong. (Acts 7:54–60)
Jesus was crucified on a cross when he didn't do anything wrong. (Luke 22–23)

Dealing with UNFAIR begins when you come to grips with that one stark, cold fact:

LIFE CAN BE UNFAIR. *(sorry)*

Moving from Unfair.

In John 13:1 it says Christ loves His followers *TO THE END*.

God doesn't want you to be SPLIT; He wants you to be Complete. And He will be with you, through everything—*TO THE END*—bringing you to the day when you are Complete. Not broken, not split, not hurting, but

COMPLETE.

That's what God wants for us.

Think of it like this...

God invites you to have an amazing life. He wants to give you incredible opportunities and challenges way beyond your capability right now. So God uses everything that happens to you—both good and bad—for this purpose. If you're SPLIT in some area, He wants to make you complete. He wants to fill you up.

And the divorce? It was someone else's choice for your life. And that wasn't fair. But God will use that huge, unfair splattered lamb of pain in your life as part of His amazing Plan to make you Complete.

SO WHAT'S YOUR DECISION?

Your decision is like this...

Now there was in Jerusalem a pool where a great number of disabled people used to lie—the blind, the lame, the paralyzed. One who was there had been an invalid for thirty-eight years. (John 5:2–6)

When Jesus saw him lying there and learned that he had been in this condition for a long time, Jesus asked him a question with

ONE OF THE MOST OBVIOUS ANSWERS EVER:

"DO YOU WANT TO BE WELL?"

How about you? Do you want to be well? Of course you do.

But sometimes you just can't see how to get well, how to let go of UNFAIR...how to be Complete.

When something bad happens to you, it's easy to feel knocked off course. But God has no Plan B for his kids. If His first best gets wasted or bloodied or splattered, you don't get His second best. He always has another first best—another Plan A. (It's called Redemption, and it's something only God can do).

From sorrow,
HE BRINGS JOY.

From loss,
HE BRINGS GAIN.

From a mess,
HE BRINGS SOMETHING BEAUTIFUL.

From the original Splattered Lamb,
HE BROUGHT AN INFINITE KING.

Your Choice: Move from Unfair and say yes to His Plan.

HE WHO BEGAN A GOOD WORK IN YOU WILL CARRY IT ON TO COMPLETION UNTIL THE DAY OF CHRIST JESUS.

(PHILIPPIANS 1:6)

I am **split**
in two

Over there
on the ground
the axe is just
lying there now
not moving.

But pieces are being
gathered up now
stacked sorted

Something more will come from all this yet

Eight things Ralph's cousin would tell you about your parents' divorce:

1. You caused it.

2. Your parents don't love you now.

3. You can never trust your parents ever again.

4. You don't have to listen to what your parents say anymore—they screwed up!

5. You'll feel a whole lot better if you start drinking a lot, or sleeping around, or cutting your arms, or fighting, or banging your head against a wall, or taking drugs, or driving really dangerously, or sinking yourself into porn, or swearing at your teachers, or stealing stuff to get attention, or doing any of the fun things that have always proven safe and effective when dealing with pain. Yep, those things always help.

6. You are the man of the house (or woman of the house) now. You run the show. It's all up to you. You have to worry about everything now, Bucko.

7. You are responsible for getting your parents back together again.

8. You are guaranteed to get divorced yourself someday.

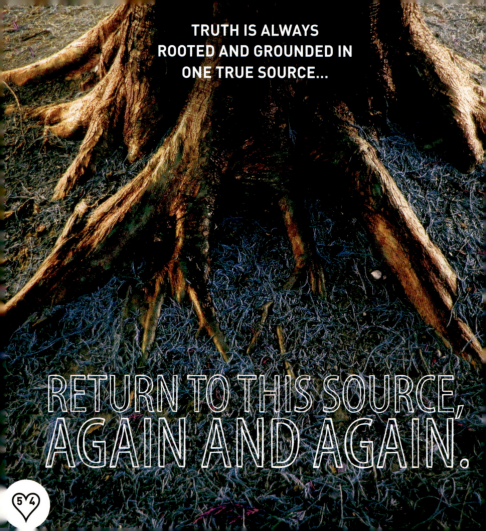

The God of all grace, who called you to his eternal glory in Christ, after you have suffered a little while, will Himself restore you and make you strong, firm and steadfast. (1 Peter 5:10)

Meaning this: Any serious hurt, like divorce, is nothing you get over in a week or two. In fact, you may feel this pain for a long time. But the great thing about Christ is this: Jesus can be the exact opposite of what you're going through.

If parents have shut you out,

CHRIST WILL LET YOU IN.

If parents are keeping secrets,

CHRIST REVEALS THE TRUTH.

When anger fills your house,

CHRIST IS PEACE.

God always keeps His promises.
God always takes care of you.
God never leaves. God is hope.

Talk to God. Tell Him everything that's going on.

Have you ever noticed that sometimes when we talk to our friends it's like...*Hey, did you know that blabber blabber blabber, and yesterday I did blabber blabber blabber*...And we just say whatever's on our minds. But sometimes when we talk to God, it's more like...*Uh sir, would You, um, bless the missionaries and my family, and thank You for this day. Amen.* God is big enough to handle anything you throw at Him. You can tell Him everything you're going through right now. *Everything.*

JUST TALK. OR YELL.

(Praying can take a lot of forms.)

Whatever your prayer looks like, or sounds like, whatever words it contains, or doesn't contain—**God can handle it.**

"If we don't know how or what to pray, it doesn't matter. [God's Spirit] does our praying in and for us, making prayer out of our wordless sighs, our aching groans." (Romans 8:26, The Message)

PRAY NOW.
PRAY ALWAYS.
KEEP PRAYING.
PRAY NOW.

Lord Jesus, help me, help us.
Help us all get through this time.
This divorce thing just hurts.
You are God. You are good.
Every day, in every way,
I'm hanging on to You.

AMEN.

FROM COACH GREEN'S PLAYBOOK
FIVE
PRACTICAL THINGS YOU CAN ALSO DO:

1. Just get through TODAY.

You might have a hundred unanswered questions in your life right now, but really, what you need to do today might look as simple as this: get out of bed, get in the shower, eat breakfast, go to school, come home, do homework, phone friends, pray, go to bed. Somehow, breaking down an overwhelming life into "today-sized" chunks can help.

2. Refuse to take sides.

You are the common link between two people who no longer want to be married. This doesn't mean you are a messenger between them or a sounding board if one parent wants to say something bad about the other. If you feel pressured to take sides, one little phrase can help. Put it in your own words, but it can be as simple as this: "Mom (or Dad), with all due respect, I love you, but I'm not going there."

3. Check the calendar.

Scheduling needs to become everyone's responsibility now. One thing that helps is a "master" calendar in each home. If you want a certain parent to attend a game or recital, make sure that parent knows about it. Make sure you tell them. Don't assume your other parent told them.

4. Remember your life too.

It's easy to get swamped with your parents' comings and goings during a divorce, and yes, this does mean you have to make a lot of concessions. It can feel like your life gets put on hold for a while, but stay focused on your own plans and dreams too. Try to stay in touch with familiar friends and do familiar activities. Eat right and get regular exercise—sounds simple, but it totally helps with the stress.

5. Don't do this alone.

Make sure you talk to someone—an older person who you trust—who's been through this before.

http://www.splitblog.com/savannahkid46/april9blog/commentsfromfriends

Comments from friends: Restoring...   April 9

At first I hated that my mom was dating again, but then I realized that she was just trying to find someone that made her feel loved and happy again. Once I started to see things from her perspective, I didn't mind her dating so much anymore. I just wanted her to find a way to be happy.

--Jordanmonk

With my parents, it was easy to feel sometimes like I was in the middle. My mom especially, would complain to me about what a rat my dad was. But I would just say to her, you need to talk to dad about that. I'd never deliver messages for them either. There was no way I was going to put myself in that position.

--Lorriezuz

I went and saw a counselor when my parents divorced. She was really nice, and we just talked and stuff. I think it helped.

--JustMeghann910

I was really stressed out before my parents split up. They fought so much it was actually a relief when Mom moved out to be with her girlfriend. I listened to music a lot then, and I wrote in my journal all the time. Sometimes I just went for a run and ran and ran.

--GenericBloggerdude

GOD'S PLAN A:

Now, and as the years go by...
You're invited to trade your rights for grace.

The hurt of a divorce is this: You were stepped on. You were the innocent party, and you got hurt. And that hurt affects a lot of your life. It can grind in you for years like gears that don't quite mesh. When we're hurt, it's easy to start listing our rights. You know—the things we're entitled to.

Like...

I have the right to be really ticked off.
I have the right to do whatever I want to do.
I have the right to make some really big mistakes right now.
I have the right to hold grudges and not forgive.

But clinging to your rights only brings you ulcers. It only hurts you.

The invitation is grace. You receive it in Christ. You extend it because He helps you to.

Grace is not the easy way out. Grace acknowledges the hurt. It says: I was wronged. But I choose to let this go. I choose to love you anyway. I choose a life of peace, not a life of rage.

I TRADE MY RIGHTS FOR GRACE.

Once I was SPLIT in two
I havent forgotten the axe
I will NEVER forget it

But somehow it is farther away from me now

Gather my pieces as a new shingled roof, sheltered, dry, safe. Gather my pieces as wooden toys, painted gifts of red, orange, yellow. Gather my pieces—heaped and crackling—blazing on the beach as a bonfire for friends.

THERE IS A BEAUTY THAT CAN ONLY COME FROM SOMETHING THAT WAS ONCE BROKEN AND IS NOW SOMETHING MORE.